The Modern Day Jabez

The Memoirs of Paula Kendrick

SHATTERED YET REDEEMED

Paula Kendrick

The
Modern Day Jabez

The Memoirs of Paula Kendrick

SHATTERED YET REDEEMED

Paula Kendrick

© 2020 by Paula Kendrick
Published by Living Water Book,
Christian Division of Butterfly Typeface Publishing House,

Little Rock, Arkansas 72201

Print Book Edition 2020

ISBN   978-1-7357073-0-3

An attempt has been made to recreate events, locales, and conversations from the author's memory of them. The events in the book are memories from the author's perspective In order to maintain their anonymity, in some instances, the names of some individuals have been changed as well as some identifying characteristics and details such as physical properties, occupations, and places of residence to protect the identities of those involved.

Scripture quotations identified are from The New King James Version® Copyright© 1982 by Thomas Nelson, Inc used by permission all right reserved

Scripture quotations identified is the New International Version, Copyright ©2011 used by permission All rights reserved

Graphics, Art, and Designs Living Water Books

Acknowledgments

Special thanks to some in my life who have been detrimental

In making me into the woman, I am today.

God, My Biological Mother, and Adoptive Mother

God, I thank you for loving me and never leaving me.

This road has been a challenging road to travel, but God, you have

always been a gentle call away. Your presence makes life's adversities a

little better to bear.

Thank you, Lord, for my mother (Pearline Lee)

who gave birth to me, and I was given life.

And my mother (Betty J Lee) for raising me, helping me through life,

nurturing, and loving me.

Dedication

My Heartbeats.
The road has not been easy, but it needed to be traveled.
You have helped me to remain humble.

Shardaye - I want to say that I love you dearly. We have both learned so much from each other. I have seen you overcome so much, and I am proud of you. Keep striving. Let God lead you.

Connie R - I want to say that I love you dearly. We have gone through some hard times together, but at the end of the day, we are still standing. Through everything, God is keeping us.

Freddy - I want to say that I love you dearly. Boy, who knew that the baby of the bunch would surely be a handful. Packing a powerful punch, I want you to know that I am so grateful for the trials.

To my daughter, Jamillia Kendrick, and my two handsome grandboys, I love you and thank you for not severing the ties because of the dissolution of the union between your father and me.

For my friend Vanessa Rodgers, who helped tremendously by giving me a journal to write all my feelings in to help cope with losing my mom, my best friend, and for getting through my divorce.

For my friend Anita Reed
You have shown me that perseverance is necessary. You have beaten the odds by being a cancer survivor, and I look at you in amazement. We are down like four flat tires without a spare and a jack, and you keep me encouraged.
I thank God for your friendship every day.

My near and dear friend Terrie Taylor aka Louise.
You have been a God Sent Angel to watch over me. You are indeed a sister's keeper. Thank you, you have motivated and encouraged me. You are the best friend anyone could ask for. You are the one who keeps it 100, and

You are brutally honest.

Each one mentioned has played a tremendous part in my life, and I love you. God puts people in our lives to be a blessing. Thanks again to all my angels for watching over me and seeing about me.

I get up every morning saying

"Continually let your light shine."
In Mathew 5:14 it says
"You are the light of the world.
A town built on a hill cannot be hidden

I no longer hide in the shadows of my hurt.

I want to be able to heal and heal others

with my story.

Author Paula Kendrick

Table of Contents

Lessons for The Soul

Foreword

When I first received the request to write the foreword, I was like, What? But as the night grew closer to an end, I said to myself, "Terrie, you know Paula, oh so well; you can do this."

I have known Paula most of her life; however, it is in the later years that we have become so close. We grew up in the same community as kids, and we now live in the same community as sisters. My sister sat out on a mission to write about her life; we rode around town and discussed it.

I wanted her to be 100% sure that she wanted to open her life for the world to see. Then Approximately a year later, another mission was accomplished by my sister. Paula has shared some very intimate details about her life, and I do not believe anyone can tell her story better than she.

Paula is a nurturer by nature, and I am more than sure this book will help someone along the way. It is through her pain that she will uplift someone else.

It is who she is and what she does.

Terry Taylor

Preface

The Modern-Day Jabez

There I was in my mother's womb, still growing pretty strong while my life was being mapped out for me. The plan to give me away for adoption had become this topic of discussion. I am inside, they're outside, and I had no input. I did not get an idea of the journey that was ahead of me. It is presumptuous how people decide on your behalf that would one day twist and turn forming into roots of pain.

"The Modern-Day Jabez" gives you a glimpse into the life of Jabez lived out through me, *Paula Kendrick*. In the Bible, 1 Chronicles 4:9,10. Jabez was born into rejection. He was more honorable than his brothers, yet his mother called his name Jabez meaning, "because I bore him in pain." But one day, Jabez called upon the God of Israel saying, "Oh, that you would bless me indeed and enlarge my territory, and that your hand might be with me.

Lord, keep me from harm so that it might not bring me pain!" God granted what he asked. Jabez's mother birthed him and named him pain. The success Jabez enjoyed with God outweighed the sorrow of his beginning.

The Memoir of Paula Kendrick is a path of suffering, success, hope, and heartache. A journey of learning God during turbulent times and understanding there is not anyone you can truly depend on in the turbulence of life but God. There I was roaming from agony while producing more anguish. I confronted a hatred I had never known from childhood into adulthood. The hatred was so cold that pieces of my soul shivered as I endured one thing after another. I traveled on for quite some time, but my "Heavenly Father" was right by my side, guiding me every step of the way.

My narrative is healing for the heart and shelter for the soul that needs strength. There is redemption after the plots and attacks against your life.

The 1st Trimester

Unborn & Underdeveloped

I knew I was different.
I knew I was special.
My name meant pain, and those
connected to me attached their pain,
but this pain was not the end for me.

Jabez was more honorable than his brothers. His mother had named
him Jabez. Saying," I gave birth to him in pain. 1 Chronicles 4:9

Chapter One

The Effects of Adoption

Unfamiliar Place of Purpose

Adoption is a process whereby a person assumes the parenting of another, usually a child, from that person's biological or legal parent or parents. Legal adoptions permanently transfer all rights and responsibilities, along with filiation, from the biological parent or parents. Nonetheless, adoption was more than an exchange for me. Let us cut the legal jargon and hear the heart of a child; it was like this unfamiliar place of rejection and emotional struggles, which slowly evolved into decisions of destruction.

There were a few seeds of rejection which became the roots within my heart. The roots traveled so deep that they began crossing over into other areas of my life. The choices of my life stemmed from the thoughts, decisions, and homes of the parents who raised me. I am in no way blaming anyone for anything, but to understand the life you will now read about, you must know what I have survived. My past predicted my future until I learned how to be transformed from the past. Before I begin, I would like to help you further understand the behaviors that became normal in my life. One behavioral pattern was too hard for me to trace until it was too late.

Throughout the chapters, there are traces of separation anxiety, which is reasoning that occurs within the mind of someone who takes so many losses as a child, something that develops and has the tendency to remain from childhood to adulthood. Most adults with a separation anxiety disorder are categorized as being controlling or overprotective. These behaviors occur often, and people refer to them as the standard. However, it is not healthy, and their actions are often an adult's way of expressing their fears regarding separation.

Symptoms would include but are not limited to

- *Unrealistic worries about the safety of loved ones,*

- *Unusual distress about being separated from a person*

- *Excessive worry that another person will be harmed if they leave them alone*

- *Heightened fear of being alone*

- *Physical symptoms when they know they will be separated from another person soon*

- *Excessive worry surrounding being alone*

- *Needing to know where a spouse or loved one is*

This disorder affects many relationships we attempt to have in life. This including adoption, parenting, transferring children, and blended families deal with this as well. The kind of results it generated in my childhood, adulthood, dating, marriage and parenting were devastating. As victims of this, we must press harder and persevere to overcome. Even Moses dealt with rejection, adoption, and separation anxiety, from Exodus 2 to Exodus 4. Then he returns not only to face his past and deal with the unfair treatment but to deliver his family all while leading them to Christ.

Moses did not know his identity or his purpose until later in life. I, just like Moses, was forced into a foreign land, where I was nurtured and taken care of by someone who was not my birth mother. Moses searched for his identity, while Jabez felt sorrow carrying the stain of pain. I became a collaboration of both. Within these pages are my chronicles, and it was through the various accounts that I learned how to catch the bricks thrown at me to build a pathway into my fate later.

Chapter Two

The Beginning

Childhood Realities

It was a hot summer morning; I was awakened by the sun shining through my window blinds and the heat hitting my skin from the sunlight. Saturday mornings were always fun for me because I could play with my Barbie dolls and then run around outside with my cousins. I jumped from the bed, ran into the kitchen, and grabbed a bowl of cereal to eat. I then put on my favorite blue jean shorts with my tie-dye colorful T-shirt. The outside was calling me for some summer fun.

"Momma, I am going outside to play." I screamed through the house!

Delana, "Wait a minute, honey, I need to tell you something, and it can't wait," Momma said.

Yes, ma'am," I replied.

So, I ran into the living room where my mom was seated, and I knelt at her feet. She said, "There is no easy way to say it." Then she calmly eased into it. "Delana, I'm not your biological mother. Your father and I adopted you before you were born. Your biological mother is Pearline."

Huh, I sat and waited; for an explanation, I was confused. Tears began to swell in my eyes, as I said, "Momma, you are the only momma I know."

"Does this mean I have to go because I have two mommies?"

Judgmental emotions consumed me, and my feelings began racing in my mind at full speed. My eleven-year-old brain could not comprehend this quick enough. I did not have a thorough understanding of what it meant to be adopted. All I knew, was the lady that I called mom did not carry me in her tummy for nine months.

My mom grabbed my hand and said, "No, you are my daughter, I am your mother, but I didn't want to go on without telling you the truth. The truth is you were a newborn baby, six weeks old, to be exact when your birth mother gave you up for adoption."

The Unexpected Twist

Delana, I am Pearline's sister in law which would initially be your aunt because your biological dad and adoptive dad are blood brothers. I was sobbing hysterically.

She cried with me, but then left me alone to think and pull myself together. I was eleven years old, but I was mature. Still a child but built with a tenacity different from most. I needed time to process. See, I always received two different versions of how the adoption took place; nonetheless, the characters of the story never change, and I was still adopted. When my adoptive mom shared her version of the truth, she told me that while my birth mom was pregnant with me, she was joking around one day and randomly said to my birth mom,

---

"You need to give me that baby, you already have eight other kids, and you don't need another one."

My birth mom told me she felt sorry for her sister in law because she could not have any children, so she decided to allow her to adopt me. I started having these thoughts in my mind telling myself who cares and ponders on the reasons behind the adoption. I knew that my birth mom did not want me (gulping down air, feeling this chunk rise in my throat, tears in my eyes running down my cheeks). The reasoning behind it did not matter to me; for that alone, I was angry.

I was so angry!

"Angry at the fact that a mother, my mother, could have eight other kids and then decide that she wanted to give me up, me... the baby out of the bunch," I said, with such a frustrated undertone.

I thought to myself, "Why not give up the 2nd, 4th, or 5th child."

Do you know how hard that was for me, thinking that I was not loved, and my very own mother who carried me for nine months did not want me? Thinking, continuously, Why Me?

Why would she do this?

Have you heard of the saying that I'm so mad that my blood is boiling? I felt this way for such a long time, even into adulthood. I literally felt HOT from the inside out! Every time I thought about it, I started to feel flushed and hot all over again because even though my biological mom thought it was a legitimate reason to give me up for adoption, my heart couldn't grasp it. Even with all the facts, there was trauma. The experience crushed me so that I said in my heart,

"If I ever have children, I will love them and never give them up for adoption. Even If life circumstances ever happened that were so traumatic and I was forced to live in a box or under a bridge, they would still be right beside me."

Pearline, my biological mom, lived right down the street from us. We did not have a close connection like a mother-daughter should; of course, I was not raised

27

by her; I didn't call her mom, but I embraced my siblings from her.

What did she want from me?

The truth was told to me, and then I was expected to be okay with it. My birth mother would host events serving dinner for the family, and it felt awkward because I had become the topic of conversation with other family members. I once overheard them whispering among themselves saying,

---

"There's the child she gave up for adoption."

It always made me feel sad and mad when people would make that statement or talk about me as though I were not there. Despite how awkward I felt, I must say, my adoptive mom and dad were loving and special. I loved them dearly. The relationship I had with my daddy was unique to my heart. God gave me 12 years with him, and I knew he loved me.

A Letter to Heaven
for My Father

Dad,

I find myself thinking of you more and more now;
I just need you to give me advice and just let me cry
on your shoulders. I miss the times of us
spending together, just sitting and being in each
other's presence. I sit here alone without you, and it
gets hard at times. I no longer have you or mom,
and my heart breaks at times.

My children never got a chance to meet you, and I
know they would be so spoiled with love and would
not want for anything because you spoiled me. A
father's love is like none other because you were a
provider and a protector. Thank you so much for
loving me in the amount of time we had with each
other.

The Tribute: A Father's Love

Love always protects, always trusts, always hopes, always perseveres. 1st Corinthians 13:7

In Loving Memory of My Father

My father was a hunter, fisherman, and just an overall outdoorsman. I think back on all the animals he would hunt, kill, and bring home. I still call myself a country/city girl if there is such a thing, because I could never hunt. However, I dearly loved to fish. I considered my dad a jack of all trades who liked to fix broken items. One day I attempted to take apart a television and tried putting it back together. I wish you could have seen me struggling. I had parts everywhere and could not put the tv back together like it once was (chuckle).

It was just fun being beside him and tinkering with gadgets. These were the precious moments between a daughter and her father. I held these memories in my heart, thinking I would get the opportunity to have more, but my adoptive dad died in a house fire trying to save a person with paraplegia when I was 12 years old. I was such a daddy's girl and losing my dad at that time (when it should have been all about him and me) was a devastating time for me. I remember running down the street, everyone standing there looking at the house burning down to the ground. This black, gray looking smoke hovered over us as the house burned. The fire department told my mom and me; there was

31

nothing they could do. My thoughts dissolved into words, and I screamed, saying, "What do you mean there is nothing you can do; you are the fire department, and you're just standing around!"

I was furious and hurt… My dad is dying, and you are not helping him. I screamed!

They were unable to get into the house and save him. I was so crushed. I could not cry, even though I needed to grieve. Family members were rushing me as they kept telling me that I needed to cry and release my hurt. Who says there is a time frame for you to grieve or a particular way to grieve? I tried to put it out of my mind but being adopted and losing a parent to death is hard. The tragedy replayed like an old sad song placed on repeat.

Singing, you will no longer see your dad anymore!

It was heartbreaking and painful. I convinced myself that if I grieved at that moment. I would have to say goodbye. I could not say goodbye, and I didn't want to let him go; I just could not let him go. My dad and I had a great relationship. It took me two weeks to finally break down and cry.

I had moments of being cold inside because my father passed on; I cherished the memories that we shared.

Chapter Three

The Evolution
Childhood to Womanhood

My life changed after the passing of my father. The years flew by like a rushing wind. I was a typical teenager trying to cope with helping my mother, tackling school exploring life, kicking it with friends, all while evolving. I became older, and I had to make sure all of my mom's affairs were taken care of; in regards to paying the bills, making sure she got to her doctor's appointments, and any other things she needed that she was not capable of doing. My momma did not have a driver's license, so my uncle and I drove her around. We struggled for years. I remember us receiving food stamp assistance, in which it is sad to say because we only received a monthly amount of $75 while being on a fixed income of social security. We experienced extreme hard times, but in our neighborhood, we grew up in, it seemed to be a typical way of living. It was ingrained within us that this is life, and we needed to be tough to survive. Life was hectic for me, but not when I hung out with my friends.

Sandra, Charlotte, and I were like the three musketeers. Sandra was the wild one; Charlotte was my cousin, but she was the quiet, level-headed one that kept us grounded. Now I was the life of the party. The one who cracked the jokes and kept everyone laughing. My friends and I were always together, and they would stay at my house. No matter how dreadful life became, I had my girls. We were ready for adulthood—living, being, and creating a path that we wanted for our own lives. Of course, we talked about our home life, education, feelings, boys, and parents. My biological mom and my adopted mom were tough subjects to discuss because there were issues from my childhood that pressed deep in my heart. No matter how many times I heard the story, I would get angry. I could not grasp how anyone could give up a child and think it was just like giving up groceries to the neighbor next door. My friends kept me calm and comfortable, but the resentment bubbled over at times. One day as I was picking out my school clothes, I heard my mother scream, "Delana, Come here. You think you grown?"

"Think you got it all figured out, huh?"

I mumbled under my breath, "Here we go again." I knew where this was headed; instead, I waited... waited to see what would make her say this, this time. She would have these outbursts of anger as if anger had a specific agenda for me. Delana, "You are going to be just like your brothers and sisters!" She said this while sipping on her ice water in her big glass mason jar. I watched her sit it down as she crunched on her ice.

All these years, I was still dealing with my sentiments regarding my birth mom. I had trapped this anger in my heart about all that happened to me and missing my daddy. She made me so mad, comparing me to my siblings, saying that I would end up like them. I do not even live with them; they are pieces of me scattered everywhere like everything else. This time I could not let it go. I am getting older, and I have my own identity. The anger started burning my chest. I felt it that even my ears were smoking. Momma, I screamed, "I am a woman with my own identity. I have my wounds and my own heart. I am not like the others."

Then I picked up that mason jar before realizing it and threw it against the wall by the front door. The glass shattered everywhere. I screamed, "Momma, I am tired of being compared to them!"

Then for a moment, everything grew; still, it even seemed like the earth just stopped moving. My anger had gotten the best of me. My mom just stopped and stared at me as my actions expressed the frustration of always being compared to others. My anger spilled over, and I was shaking inside, but outwardly I just stood still. I had nothing left to give. I felt low. Then the more she stared at me, the more I saw comfort overtake the fear in her eyes; that comfort within her helped me to calm down.

"Momma," I said, "Please forgive me. I apologize." She smiled and apologized too. She agreed that she would never say it again

In my mind, I said over and over my mom is hindering and stifling me. She was over-protective of me and stunting my growth. However, I lost my daddy, and she lost a husband; The smart comments that spiraled out of control was also her grief. The truth is she was there for me like none other. I was mature enough to know that it was to be expected. My momma walked me right through adolescence, then propelled me into womanhood. She shared knowledge with me that went beyond the simple things of life. *Boys would say, "My daddy talked with me about the birds and the bees!!"*

This topic is usually about life and sex. Well, my momma taught me about the *flames, flowers, and the fleas.* This topic is about the hard-rough areas of life, the pretty beautiful and blossoming moments in life, and watch out for the things that try to attach itself to you like fleas to an animal. We discussed a lot, but there was one area of my heart I had not rendered.

I threw the rules out the window and embraced the ending of my twelfth-grade year with a goal—the goal of turning a life of empty promises into a life of security and love.

The 2nd Trimester

The Maturation Process

Father lead me as a good father does.
When I cry to you of my troubles,
You are there to protect me.

Let your hand be with me and keep me from harm so that I will be free from pain." And God granted his request. 1 Chronicles 4: 10b

Chapter Four

From the Friend Zone to Marriage
The Beautiful Blossoming Flower

I met Sonya at the age of 3 years old. We were what you would call baby buddies. She and I were close friends. I would go over to her house, and she'd come by mine. We would play games, have deep conversations, and in those times, I would always see her brother Larry. He was like a brother because his sister was like my sister until my fall semester. It was the year of 1988, my senior year of high school at Wilbur D Mills became the year I would never forget. Eighteen years old and I was flirting with my future, I was ready for something to blossom into more than just a bud. My body was screaming for the attention of my best friends' brother.

43

In my mind, we were not babies anymore, and I wanted him. He was older and experienced, and I was young and excited. I tried to find any reason to get to their home, but my momma was still momma.

Did she know my plan?

Did she know I had a crush on him?

Did she find my notebook with all the hearts around his name? She made it her business to keep me at home and let me invite Sonya to our house. I would typically see Larry in passing, but days went by, and I had not seen him.

I was gazing out of my window, looking across the neighborhood, hoping to see his car pass. Just love-struck, giggling and blushing as I replayed that statement in my head, repeatedly. I would laugh at myself because I did not know if he wanted me the way I wanted him. He had his grown man on. You know what I mean, the kind of man that always had money, gas in his car, hard worker. Yeah, a real man.

Senior skip day was just a day away, and I know my momma had to go to a convention. I made plans to stay around my best friend as much as possible. I went to my closet and pulled out my cutest gear.

I even wanted my clothes to grab his attention. I was so excited I could not sleep, but I did. I needed a refresher by morning. My alarm clock went off, the smell of love hit my nose, and I was out of bed getting dressed. In order for senior skip day to look legit, I needed to leave at the scheduled time of my regular departure. I promised Sonya I'd meet her at her home.

"Momma, I screamed!" "I'm gone. I will see you after school."

She said, Okay, but my excitement was louder than her goodbye. I let the screen door slam, and I walked for 3 minutes to my best friend's house. I crossed the street, and under the oak tree was Larry bent over in his car. My stomach started turning flips. I was trying to calm myself down, but I couldn't. I was getting ready to come face to face with Larry, and no one was outside, but he and I. I played it cool, hoping he would say something to me but pretending like I didn't see him at all. Finally, he stood up, put his hands and arms on the roof of his car, then watched me as I walked by.

"Lana, it's senior skip day, what's up," Larry said.

Smiling inside while blushing outwardly, I stammered a bit with my words. Hmm, you tell me what's up?

He walked towards me. I put my hands on my hips and popped my gum. He whispered, "you look good today!"

I stepped back then said, Thank you. So, do you... The door started creaking as it swung open wide. It was my best friend, Sonya. Larry started backing away and making jokes to his sister. I needed to find another way to spend just a little bit more time together, so I said, Uh Ummm. Sonya and I need a ride; we can't miss hanging out with everyone today. Laughing at my efforts, He walked over to his orange 1970ish Monte Carlo. I called it the Dukes of Hazzard car because the door on the passenger side did not open.

Then he told us to get in. We had to climb in through the window to get into the car, which I always thought was cool anyway, so there was no shame. I figured this would be the perfect time for him to get one more good look at me before this moment came to an end. He drove us to the center station, and we said our goodbye's,

"Lana," Larry said, "I'll see you."

I just turned around and smiled. I dated other guys before him, but Larry was my dream guy.

He was older than me, so I had to be smart about dating him. Sonya asked "Girl, you really like my brother huh?"

I laughed; she's my best friend. I couldn't lie to her, so I admitted it. Yes, girl. I said, "he's better than peanut butter and jelly. He always has money, always doing odd jobs, among other things, and I want to be his wife."

My best friend screamed, girl, that's gross. He is my brother. We laughed it off, but I planned to be with him after graduation, and that was in just a few days. After all the festivities, Sonya and I arrived home. We made it no further than the patio when the mail carrier ran.

My cap and gown had arrived in the mail. I tore through the packaging, and I tried it on just to see how it would look. Graduation was approaching, job applications needed to be considered I created all these plans and ideas in my mind with my future wrapped around one man. Excited about my new journey, but sad about all the memories I'd leave behind.

"Lana!" Sonya Shouted. 'Where were you just now?"

I mean, I called your name a thousand times; why didn't you answer? She knew I would daydream at any given moment, but this time she is shouting startled me. I looked at her with a blank stare and asked, did you really have to yell?

"Girl, I am thinking about life after graduation."

Sonya, what do we do next? We have made so many memories, and now we have to start new ones? Sonya looked at me with this sadness in her eyes. Finally, the only words she could muster up were Lana, you are right, but guess what we can be roommates in college, we can have the same classes. Life does not end when we graduate; it is just the beginning.

I said within myself, she got plans for me, I got plans for me, and momma got plans for me.

Did anyone ask me what I wanted to do with my life?

I knew this conversation was the start of something more. The more I thought about it, the more I realized I had no reason to be sad. Larry was going to be my husband and Sandra, my sister. My cheeks turned upward as my tassel flew in my eyes. I will always have a family. Just a few days and This walk across this auditorium will be the beginning of the rest of my life.

The Possibilities

Graduation Day was finally here, and people filled the bleachers. People arrived to see us release those caps in the sky and soar just as high as those caps. This was it. The last day I would be a girl and the first day that I step into the new day as a woman. They called my name, and this accomplishment was my own success story. Growing up without and finding out I was adopted, then handed over to be raised by others, feeling awkward around my siblings because they don't seem like siblings at all but strangers, enduring the loss of my father and remembering all the times my adopted mom said mean things.

My doubts, discouraging conversations flashed in my face, yet I stood up proud. Proud to walk in liberty at the sound of my name. I graduated with a 3.0 GPA; I was determined to be better than what others thought. All my family was sitting in those stands, but I still felt alone. I suppose I was so ready for this day so I could define my own life. The labels of life became exhausting, and I wanted to prove to myself that I wasn't a mistake. I dragged these strings of lies around for so long, but today as I pulled my tassel from one side to the other. It was my time to create another one.

My future was in front of me, my boyfriend next to me with children on the horizon. We moved in together after graduation. I heard love songs, lyrics dancing in my head. He heard convenient sex. Either way, we were together.

Right or Wrong? I had control of my life, and it felt good to be grown and in control. We lived in a trailer park—this spacious two-bedroom mobile home with my momma. Everything was good for a while until I started noticing things I had not seen before. Larry was slowly changing, but I kept giving more of myself. I needed him to know I was in love with him, and I wanted children with him. I wanted a life with him, so I started taking liquid Geritol; I heard it could help with fertility. There I was gulping it down like it was a cool, refreshing soda on a hot summer's day.

All I knew was,

Delana, (me) was all grown up. I chuckled as I reminded myself that I was not a little kid anymore. I really wanted to be someone's mother. There were so many longing aches that came with being rejected, adopted, and unaccepted as a child. This ache was one of many aches. I felt like I needed a child to complete me. I thought to myself, Larry needs to understand that this was a plan, and it is our plan now. Our child would never have to worry because I would not repeat the actions of my mother. I was startled from my long talks in my heart when I heard my name.

"Lana, Come Here," Larry shouted. There I came running. "Larry, why did you scream my name?"

He looked at me and said, I just wanted you. I smiled.

He reached for me. I leaned in to kiss him, and I promise it felt like the 4th of July with fireworks bursting outward everywhere. He and I made love. I wanted to have his baby, and I did. I counted down the months like crazy. We were preparing for our child, enjoying the kicks in my womb. Nine months and there she was We gave birth to our first baby girl on April 17, 1991. We named her Lisa Marie, and she was a dream come true. I am a mother.... motherhood was happening for me!! I had lullabies bouncing around in my head, and I began singing. During the songs, I began to wonder, did someone think this way about me when I was born? I took a long look at our baby and said, "I'm going to be the best mother ever, and no one will hurt you, You will never experience pain. You will know joy. You will be full of joy." I was determined to make sure she did not see pain, so I became overprotective incredibly early.

I had labels of rejection, pain, and being a mistake embedded in my soul that I still related myself to JABEZ from birth. However, I didn't want that curse over my baby head. I knew about Jabez and Moses from my childhood, learning about them in Sunday school. I related myself to them both because they felt pain. I remember thinking that was me. My mind wandered off into this sea of darkness. Pain flooded my heart, but when I looked back at our baby girl, I said, "You will never experience pain, Lisa Marie." "I am never leaving you."

Larry knew my pain because I confided in him over the years. He knew how important becoming pregnant meant to me. I fell in love with him more for giving me what no one else could. He gave me reasons to live. The sweet aroma of our baby was like this fresh bottle of baby lotion. It was springtime in my arms, and I knew it.

"Larry, we have our baby," I exclaimed.

He looked, smiled so hard then said. "Yeah, we did it Lana, we did it together." We were so happy that we started building a future together. We weren't married yet, but I had one part of my plan complete, and I was delighted. We watched our baby girl grow.

We moved out of momma's house and into the trailer right behind my momma. If she walked out of her back door, and I walked out of my front door, laughing, we were right there to meet up in the middle of the pathway. This set up was so convenient for Larry and me because I still had them both, and my momma could see her grandchild anytime. Larry and I were inseparable. One evening while momma was visiting, she said, Larry can't do anything without having you under him. He always calls you, and you are always running to him. I said, "Momma, that is not true."

But she was right, and no matter how much I wanted to admit she was wrong, I couldn't help myself. Of all the people I met in my life, I was strongly attracted to him. He had this hold on me. I found someone who wanted me for me, and it felt good to be desired and liked.

"Lana, Lana!" Larry screamed, "Come here."

I was cooking dinner, and momma just laughed as she thought it was funny. I ran right to him. Who was I kidding? Just a girl in love with the guy of her heart. Larry was a real outdoorsman, usually tinkering outside with a car, cutting the lawn, washing the vehicles, or something. He loved getting his hands dirty, and I was fascinated by that because this separated the professionals from the amateurs. A man with dirty hands was such a turn on, so if he were outside, he would call me, and I'd come running.

Then we fell on hard times,

We went from happy and enjoying each other to walking on rocky shaky grounds. We were always arguing about something. I thought I could change all the things I did not like about Larry. I thought having a baby would make me happy and bring us closer together; I ignored the red flags and pushed passed them because of love.

Don't we as women think that? I worked odd jobs (temp jobs) and purchased multiple items for him to show how much I cared. Why do we, as women, have to facilitate and validate in ways of gifts? I was buying gifts, and he was mistreating me, falling in love and out of love. I became pregnant again. When our eldest daughter was four years old, we had another baby. Our 2nd girl was born on January 26, 1995, and she came out looking just like her daddy. We named her LaRae because she should've been a junior. They looked like twins.

Immediately following the birth of our baby girl, Larry began having health issues. He was in such agony and pain we immediately rushed him to the hospital. The doctors needed to do immediate surgery because He had hyperthyroidism. I was worried and scared for him. I stayed at the hospital at night while my mom took care of the babies. It was there in the hospital that the most thoughtful, loving surprise came from his mouth.

"Lana," Larry said, "You've been by my side through all of this. I cannot repay you for the way you've committed yourself to me even during this injury. You have sacrificed for me. I care about you, and I just think we need to get married." My mouth fell open in pure shock.

Was this happening?

Did he just propose?

Wait a minute. Was that a proposal?

Larry, did you just propose to me? Are you Sure? I wondered was it him I heard or the medication because it was not romantic to me; It just sounded like Larry being Larry talking.

Then he looked at me and said, "Lana, I'm serious." "Let's get married." I paused for a while, then I said, "yes!"

He grabbed my hand, and I found comfort in his eyes. We remained in the hospital for at least three more days, then began his rehab toward recovery. The road to recovery and the path to marriage felt like the same thing. He was recovering from physical injuries while I was recovering from the bumpy road of dating that led us here. Despite those feelings, invitations were sent to the immediate family, and I finally concluded that I was making the right decision.

This was my dream, right? The truth is it was my dream that was becoming a reality.

We married on August 26, 1995, at First Baptist Church Higgins in Higgins, Arkansas.

My mothers were both in attendance, and our daughters looked so beautiful, walking down the aisle. At this point in my life, I believed I reached this natural fulfillment because I had everything I wanted. I accomplished what I thought was a success, which was different from my childhood. Larry and I continued to extend our family. We gave birth to another baby girl five years later, on September 15, 2000.

Chapter Five

Cut from the Same Cloth

Marriage and Motherhood

As the years passed by, Larry and I were beginning to go in opposite directions of life; we were still married and living together. The happiness within our marriage started dissolving, and our children were feeling the effects of it throughout our home. Larry and I had three living daughters, and we endured two miscarriages.

Our girls were existing and functioning through the dysfunctional emotional instability of our marriage. I didn't think it affected them until I began to see changes in their behaviors. They were scared and anxious many times because the arguments were catastrophic. Our children would pull the covers over their heads and pray for the disagreements to cease.

We all longed for the calmness of the atmosphere to return to a sense of normalcy.

It was as though we could never get on the same page. My husband had some issues that he never wanted to deal with, and I think that made him feel insecure and uncertain at times. The more I pushed him into letting me try to help him; it infuriated him. I overlooked so many issues I honestly didn't understand the severity of the situation because I wanted Larry, and no matter what I needed to do to have him, I did it. I was slowly paying for the mistakes I made. No one taught me what to look for in a man. I was so eager to love and be loved; I thought love alone could keep any relationship going. I knew I had enough passion for both of us. He would never feel rejected like me, and I would always be needed.

This plan of mine put me in charge, with everyone relying on me. It seemed ideal until I started seeing his flaws surface. Unfortunately, I created a plan without God.

Raising Versions of Myself

It was not easy at all raising girls while dealing with my separation anxiety, marital problems, and working. I wanted to know the movement of my girls, cautious about whose house they would visit, and who their friends were.

Sounds familiar?

Yes, I was repeating a cycle that I could not break. I thought I was sheltering my children from pain and heartache, but agony greeted them in every corner of our home. This agony included my mental illness from my adoption and the effects it had on my actions toward my children. I also began seeing similar traits of my behaviors within our children. I was always the disciplinarian in our marriage, which made me look like I was the enemy in the eyes of our children.

This role alone caused me to face rejection that I had not dealt with since childhood. The dismissal was a reminder of loneliness and feared seeing it with my children caused tension to be so thick it filled the air and lingered in the walls.

Our daughter, Lisa Marie, and LaRae, literally wanted to walk through our wall rather than pass by me in the hallway in fear of brushing up against me. That was both hurtful and hard. Now, do you see how unresolved childhood issues surface in our adult life? This monster followed me, and now it was rearing its ugly head again only through my children. I was feeling so depressed, and I started experiencing suicidal thoughts; knowing that my child hated me was incredibly challenging for me. This cycle erupted again. What was I doing wrong? I wondered,

"Is this how my biological mother felt?"

I mean, this was not the same thing, right? At least this is what I told myself over and over. I was the victim, and I did not deserve the treatment of being rejected. I released a deep moan and sigh; I needed it to end, but how do you stop something you have never confronted. Unfortunately, our children felt the same way, and I was helpless. When you feel as though you are doing everything for your child, they turn around and have so much animosity towards you; it is heartbreaking. I not only had to deal with children and their attitudes, but I also had to deal with the fact that my husband and I argued quite a bit. Well, let's be realistic, making the statement quite a bit is a compliment; it was HORRIBLE! Yes, all caps because our turmoil hindered me from being an efficient parent. We were engulfed in despondency, and chaos took control. These emotions began to erupt like a volcano through the heart of our daughter, Lisa Marie.

Lisa Marie was in junior high. One day she was late coming home, and I was so worried that I called the police to meet me at the school. Her dad nor I heard from her. We searched for her. Do you have any idea what it is like to grow up as I did then have children, only to lose one? I could not stop the thoughts from whirring like a whirlwind. "Find my baby," I screamed, "Find her!"

Then after hours of searching and crying. We found her. She was alive and well, completely feeling herself as my grandmother would say. She left the school, walking on a trail with some friends. When we arrived back at the school to get her, I said. "Lisa Marie, what has gotten into you?" This girl was trying my patience. She just rolled her eyes and said, "I didn't think it was a big deal for me to be a little late."

"Really, why are y'all so worried because I'm fine. I am sorry for not calling, but I do not know why you are tripping so hard. I wasn't kidnapped or anything. I just looked at her, wanting to discipline her so bad I could not bring myself to do it."

As her mother, I was angry and sad, but she was okay. Lisa was the defiant one. You know the child that's disrespectful because they think the world revolves around themselves. This sense of entitlement causes them only to see one aspect of life. We tried to prevent certain behaviors, so we took her to tour the juvenile detention center. The adolescent stages of life were hectic, and I had no more patience with this child. I did not know what to do, nor did I believe in counseling. No therapist was going to tell me what to do and be in my business, I thought. Then again, in this situation, we needed it. Larry checked out of our marriage and parenting emotionally and mentally, leaving me to clean up the spilled milk of our lives.

I was alone, but trouble and Lisa didn't stop hanging together. Lisa invited trouble to our front door.

Skipping school, she thought I was a Fool

It was the end of her 9th-grade year, and this little girl was missing more days of school than she was attending. Now, out of all of these days, weeks, and months, no one bothered to contact me and inform me to let me know she had accumulated these absences. I was speechless because every morning I was dropping my daughter off in front of the school at the front door. I remember the day I went to get the mail out of the mailbox, a letter from her school staring me in my face. I opened the letter up so fast, and to my surprise this letter said

Attention, Parents of Lisa Marie Your daughter has missed over 90% of the average days of school. She needed to return for Summer School to complete the 9th grade.

I was livid!!

I asked myself, how in the world does a child of mine, whom I take to school every day, have to repeat the 9th grade due to attendance?

"Lisa Marie, I was dropping you off in front of the school on my way to work every morning, you better talk and explain where you have been!" "Momma, I apologize," she said. "I don't know why I did it."

I said, "Yeah right, Lisa Marie. I'm not paying for this catastrophe. I refuse to pay for you to go to school."

"Mom," she said, "I can go to another school."

I could not believe she offered this as an option. "You most certainly cannot and will not be attending another school." I said, "you made this bed, so lie in it." After hearing this sob story, which I didn't believe, her dad felt empathy for her and paid for her to go to summer school. Our children studied us long and hard enough because they knew which parent they could get over on. I even felt as though they were pinning us against each other. "Larry, are you going to pay this?" He just stared at me with this emptiness as if he could care less what I thought. I was furious!

"You know, Larry, I don't care one way or another I am not paying for it. She is to be held accountable for her actions." It was hard for me to understand paying over $250 for a two-week summer school education when you were getting the same curriculum previously for free. This situation, along with many others, was the downfall in our marriage.

Three weeks later our other daughter became challenging, acting nonchalant and always saying, "I don't care." I was so sick of dealing with nasty attitudes. She was spewing out the hurt and pain that occurred within the walls of our home. I said, "This is what happens when you don't deal with issues, Larry."

Larry didn't care... just looked and kept going. Our daughter seemed to have looked at their sisters' actions and decided to travel the same path. Our daughters showed us that Larry and Lana were raising and parenting in pain. I had my ups and downs with Lisa Marie, but she was a walk in the park compared to LaRae. I cried on multiple occasions from being disrespected, humiliated, and brought to shame. She began befriending girls in school who would teach her how to live an inappropriate lifestyle. They had more influence in her life than I had, so I put her out of my house when she was a junior in high school. From there, she went to live with another family member for about a year and a half.

I started thinking about the decisions of my mothers. Thinking I had no right to be so angry about decisions I couldn't comprehend until now. The roles of being a wife, mother, and work a full-time job were more than I bargained for. These roles had challenges and sleepless nights—more work than I cared to give my mothers' credit for. I felt a sincere regret in the pit of my stomach. They had every right to decide adoption for me and to give me up to a family; my biological mother knew there was more I needed that she could not give. They didn't explain that to me then, but maybe if they had, I wouldn't be where I am now. I was just sick to my stomach.

My family started dissolving

When I kicked our daughter out of the house, Larry was upset, to say it mildly. LaRae was his heart, and she could not do any wrong in his eyes, nor could anyone say anything negative about her. Fighting her was like fighting him. This time was horrible in my life. I would see her in different places, and she would not speak to me. She would walk past me as though she did not see me.

LaRae, please do not act this way! I exclaimed, but she would keep walking. Years passed, and I allowed her to come back to our home, even though our relationship had not mended. My daughter moved back home during her senior year of school. She came home with changed behavior, and I was excited to have her back home. I missed her. We started hanging out together, laughing, and talking. We were repairing our relationship, and it was all going well until the unthinkable occurred.

One Friday night, I thought of her and headed for her room to check on her. I opened the door, and I did not see her there. I checked under the bed and in the closet, which was strange and odd. I remember thinking, where could she be? I looked again and did not see her. Then as I was about to lay back down, something came over me to walk to the front door. Surprisingly, the front door was locked from the inside with the deadbolt on it. That told me that she was in the house somewhere but where?

At this point, I wanted to know where she was and if she left out of the house, and if not, then how did she get out. So, I went and looked again and still did not see her and headed back into my bedroom to ask Larry if he knew anything. I heard this loud bang about 30-45 minutes later towards the back end of the house where the girl's bedrooms were. I jumped abruptly; it scared me. The noise sounded like a crash against our house. I instantly ran to their rooms, and LaRae was climbing through the window.

I said, "What the H... are you doing coming through that window and where the F... have you been. Girl, get out of my house, and don't you come back." Larry said, "You can't put her out, and where is she going?"

I said, "Larry, at this point, I do not care. LaRae, you have 24 hours to figure it out." LaRae, my nonchalant child, kept this self-absorbed (selfish attitude), she said, "I do not care what you think, nor do I care about what you want to do." I had a headache, trying to understand why she would go in and out of the window.

- ✓ *Why not use the front door?*
- ✓ *What would possess you to go through all of this when you are grown?*
- ✓ *Why would you move back into the house to do something crazy like this?*

After this, I asked her to leave again, she went and got an apartment, and she remained on her own. Larry and I could not agree on our marriage. We could not agree on being emotionally, mentally, or sexually involved. We couldn't even decide on healthy parenting habits. The battle was on-going, and I could not take it anymore.

I could not take the way my life was going anymore, and I wanted to die. The thought of suicide seemed simpler because the pain was so unbearable. I begin trying to convince myself that my mom could raise my children, and they would be better off without me. I entered a dark place; I started dancing with the devil. My pain had become the tears pouring out of my eyes. I opened the door for the devil to enter in, and he did. I was going to take my life, and I premeditated countless ways to do it.

The husband and children I worked hard to obtain... I was losing them. I was losing me. One more breath, and that's it. Satan had won from the beginning of my life until now. He beat me, and I knew it, But....

Then the light spilled into my bedroom. It had the tint of purple and blue with a white light bursting through. I was looking at myself through a reflection. I was looking at myself sitting on the side of the bed, looking into the bright light. This light had drawn me in, and I felt this peace surge through me. It was the most beautiful light ever, and I saw this silhouetted figure of a man. His body was blowing in the wind while he was standing still. I was fascinated, and he uttered these words,

Stop; your life is precious; you need to be here for your children. Get up, Now be restored. The wind blew into my mouth, my ears, my soul, and I began gasping for air. The wind was overwhelming, and my body could not contain the power. He said you have people depending on you, and they need you. Listen to me, My Beloved, you have a story to tell and work to do.

The lights absorbed into one another, and the silhouette disappeared, but he left his peace. I felt it, and in that instance, I knew that I was going to be okay. I laid back down, and when I woke up the next morning, I felt better. *Isaiah 41:10 says: Fear not, for I am with you; be not dismayed, for I am your God; I will strengthen you, I will help, I will uphold you with my righteous right hand (NIV).*

I did not fear anything because God spoke to me. It was God, he came to me, and he was preparing me for what was on the horizon. I was just amazed that I encountered God, and I heard his voice so clearly, as though he was right in front of me. I experienced the goodness of God. That was a turning point for me to make sure that I could hear and discern His voice. I asked God to deliver me and help me get through that season. I used to tell my children that I was their mother and not their friend, I had a job to do, and my mind said, do it. When the Lord calls me home, my desire is for Him to say, well done, Paula, thou good and faithful servant; that is how I always looked at it. I repeatedly ask myself, "God are you pleased with me as a parent"?

God trusts me with our children, and I cannot disobey him. Our children were the heartbeats of marriage whom God gave us stewardship over

The ages of our children during the writing of this memoir, including the miscarriages, are as follows: 28 (living), 27 (miscarriage), 24 (living), 20 (miscarriage), and 18 (living).

The 3rd Trimester

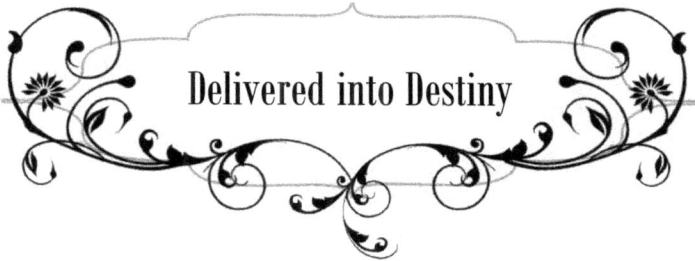

Delivered into Destiny

Father, can you hear me. Let my cup
overflow with blessings and Open doors
that man cannot shut and Shut doors
that man can't open. Let me be known
locally, globally, and internationally

Jabez cried out to the God of Israel, "Oh, that you would bless me
and enlarge my territory! 1 Chronicles 4: 10a

Chapter Six

Death Comes in Many Forms

Divorce and Death of a Friend

I had officially made up my mind to leave Larry, but I wanted to help him cope with our separation. Even after the tears and pain, I cared for him; nevertheless, he did not want my help, and I believe it was due to him being prideful, thinking I would never leave

The truth is he was right about that for many years. On numerous occasions, I tried to go, but couldn't until now. My life could no longer be this life of rejection, anxiety, pain, insecurity, seeking love, and performing for acceptance. I wanted love from a man that I thought I knew.

I interacted with him, slept beside him, all while never knowing his real thoughts toward me. When life begins with rejection, it can cause a person to start creating their own happily ever after. The images I planted in my head about us were real to me. I built this false sense of love because I never came face to face with the little girl within me who was traded off from person to person. I prayed long and hard about my marriage, and the Lord gave me a vision, and that is when I knew it was time for me to leave. In my dream, I, my husband, and our youngest child were in a car together. My husband was driving the vehicle; a tornado began forming. It started approaching us.

The faster we drove, the more the tornado was following. I told my ex to pull over because I saw a ditch or a culvert for us to get in. He pulled the car over, my baby girl and I got out of the car and got in the ditch. I begin yelling at him to get out of the car and get in the gutter. The tornado was coming. There were other people in this ditch with me as well. I was holding a baby girl in my arms very tight and had my eyes closed. When I opened them, I asked this man who was beside me if my ex was gone and he had said yes.

I knew in that instance that it was just going to be our children and me. I had just received my confirmation. The very next week, I went to file for a divorce. It was a long process and even more bitter at times; I stood in our home and finally acknowledged my fears that created this reality. Larry had this smirk on his face as I gathered the pieces of what was left. We were over, and while I was trying to make sure he was okay, he blurted the words that etched themselves within my heart like daggers.

"Lana, I never loved you!!"

The words felt like a devastating bombshell dropped on me. The fixtures in my hand fell, and I turned around with question marks in my eyes. "Larry, what do you mean you never loved me? You say this now?"

Lana, "I did not love you on our wedding day, but I grew to love you. I married you because you were there for me when I had my major surgery. You took care of me, and I realized, hmm, maybe she is in my corner after all. You are crazy to think that I loved you. I was growing to love you."

I could not understand him. I asked over and over, "How could you?"

"Why would you do this to me? Did I deserve this? Did you think this little of me? I was a charity case to you, huh Larry? I wasted all these years."

"Lana, no," he said, I just wanted to be close to my children."

Larry, this is the most deceptive and misleading thing you could ever tell me. Twenty years of my life wasted, and the truth is I knew he was right. I felt deceived, manipulated, and stripped of any rights I had to my own life and decisions. I just wanted him to love me. I replayed the moments of my life with him, and as I rehearsed it, the truth was there all along. I just never wanted to see it. I was the one making all the moves, buying everything, making sacrifices, taking care of the children. Yes, he worked, but we never had a partnership. It was there, right there. The truth had come to light, and all I could do was scream.

Why do you feel the need to mess up someone's life with your selfish ways? He said, "Lana, I love you now." Truthfully, there was no difference in what I saw then and now. Love was just another word. No actions changed, and No affections improved. That was the truth I needed, but it came at a cost.

It broke me and destroyed everything I had ever known about love. I had questions after questions that I kept asking myself.

Why not just take this truth to your grave? What happens when the relationship you longed for makes you physically sick? When you have multiple aches and pains within your body? What happens when the mutual level of respect and love you used to have is no longer there? When other people's opinions outweigh the words you have spoken to forsake one another? Do you question God when you pray to him for answers and clarity, and he gives you the means to leave?

Why not tell me this initially and let me decide if I wanted to marry you, Larry, was the question I asked myself.

God knew that the season had come where I needed to hear the truth and deal with it. I felt that my entire life had been a lie; all my choices measured up to failure. I kept hearing God say, do not lean to your own understanding. *Trust in the Lord with all thine heart; and lean not unto thine own understanding.*

In all thy ways acknowledge him, and He shall direct thy paths (Proverbs 3:5,6 NKJV). I could not get past this man masking his truth, causing me to choose him because I thought he had chosen me. I felt numb and nauseous with this news. I was just like Jabez born into pain, and pain chose me; but even in the pit of despair, God is with me. I started spending more time with God and studying to see where I went wrong in my life. I blamed Larry enough, and now it was time for me to pick up the pieces. God showed me *Ecclesiastes 4:9-12 Two are better than one because they have a good return for their labor: If either of them falls, one can help the other up. But pity anyone who falls and has no one to help them up. Also, if two lie down together, they will keep warm. But how can one keep warm alone? Though one may be overpowered, two can defend themselves. A cord of three strands is not quickly broken (NIV).*

This scripture confirmed what I already knew. God was not in our relationship, and if he had been, it wouldn't have deteriorated. I stayed on my knees for so long my carpet started forming in the shape of my body. Our lawyers' court date scheduled, the divorce was approaching, and I was struggling to maintain. Financially, I was drowning, between my mom, the payday loans, and creating tabs at an old friend's grocery store. I was borrowing money to buy groceries, borrowing money to pay bills. I was trapped, but my daughters and I were surviving. Over a year, I owed the grocery store over 95% of my entire income tax check. I had become a single mother learning the hard knocks of life.

From Divorce to Tragedy

Shortly after my divorce with Larry, my best friend Debra Johns Moore, whom I had worked with for 16 years, died. In December of 2015, the same month I was going through my divorce, she was about 30-40 minutes late for work, and I knew something was wrong. I just knew it because of her patterns. When I arrived at her apartment, I saw her car, so I ran to the door. I banged on the door, but no one came.

I called the apartment complex for the landlord to open the door. When the landlord got there, she ran back out and told me to call 911. There my friend of 16 years was lying on the floor unconscious. We were just together 24 hours before her death laughing and clowning together.

83

She was my friend, more like a sister. We would always let each other know if one of us couldn't be at work. She was there to hear me talk about my children, my ex-husband, and more intimate moments of my life. My sister was a shoulder to lean on, an arm to offer a hug, and an inspirational quote offering words of encouragement.

I Died Too

December 15' 2015, the divorce was final, and then my best friend died on the 18th. I believe I cried every day from that point on into 2016. I had fallen on my knees plenty of times to ask God to help me get through. Always telling people, I am fine, and all the while, I was corroding dying from the inside out.

I stopped wanting to go to church because I was too afraid of what everyone had to say, eyes watching me, and I could not take it. I could not muster up worship or praise anyway. Let's face it, the devil wiggled in and worked on my mind to keep me from depending on the Lord. I needed to heal and remove myself out of the way so I could grow. Death found me, stripped me, and revealed who I am in God.

84

I had to lose some things (pride, selfishness) to be called a child of God. *Ephesians 4:22-24 NIV says: That, in reference to your former manner of life, you lay aside the old self, which is being corrupted in accordance with the lusts of deceit, and that you be renewed in the spirit of your mind, and put on the new self, which in the likeness of God has been created in righteousness and of the truth.*

The death I encountered was dying to self. The divorce, depression, death, decisions all led to me finding myself. I went from shattered to redeemed. In God, I began to mature more, and I understood that every turn I made wasn't someone else's fault. I was just as at fault as others because I allowed my hurt to make decisions for me. Jabez territory became enlarged. Moses had the closest relationship with God, and God called him a friend. This depiction of their lives gives insight as to what God has in store for me.

Chapter Seven

A Mother's Love

My Rock

D o you know how hard it is to be physically looking at your mom lying in a hospital bed and not able to speak a word? One day she was talking and laughing, thinking she would be getting out of the hospital soon, and the next not able to murmur a word. There I was standing looking at my mother with tears running down her face. It was unbearable. I looked at her face then into her eyes. I knew what she was thinking and wanting to say to me. I wiped the tears from her face and reassured her that we would be okay. I believe she knew at that moment that she was dying and as a selfless act of a mother, still be concerned for her daughter.

My mom (adoptive) died on September 1, 2012, and it was hard because she was my rock. When she died, I felt so alone. I realized that my mom had done so much for my family, and she was a true monarch of whom I leaned on tremendously.

I used to call her every day to check on her. My mom and I were so close that I literally finished her sentences for her and could even predict what she would say before she said it. She had numerous medical issues that caused her to need a pacemaker. She had leg surgery to clear up some blockage, but she never recovered. She was the one I went to when I was low on money, and I would borrow money until payday to pay a bill or to get something the girls needed. If I lacked food, she was the one who provided at times. God knew that I had to bury my mom and not the other way around. My mom would not have been able to handle it if she had to bury me first. I did not even know the strength I had or needed to have until I lost her. God was with me to keep me sane during this time. It is hard to lose a parent, especially when you have such a close relationship with them. Throughout my life, I have learned how to endure losing people I loved.

Tribute to My Adopted Mother

*Because everyone who uses proverbs will use this
proverb about you: Like mother, like daughter
Ezekiel 16:44*

In Loving Memory of My Mother

I've had some hard times. I've been shattered, discarded, and life bruised my heart. Devastation and divorce nearly destroyed me, but I survived. I triumphed even the most difficult challenges. I'm a living testament to joy and healing. I need you to know I understand your decisions because you did what you thought was best. Thank you for protecting me, loving me, and saying YES to God to get me here on earth.

I was Shattered now. I'm Redeemed.

Conclusion

In the memoirs of my life, *Shattered Yet Redeemed*. I found myself while writing this book. I released answers throughout the chapters. I needed God to intervene, and it was there in the scriptures that he revealed Jabez to me. God needed me to get out of my way to enlarge my territory. My pain was not the stopping point, but it did provide detours in my life. Those detours unveiled the scales of darkness that became interwoven into my heart. I was making decisions based upon the familiar. I forgave my past, and I forgave myself.

Now forgive yourself....

How do you begin to heal?

Cry out to the Lord and ask him to help.

"So do not fear, for I am with you; do not be dismayed,
for I am your God. I will strengthen you and help you;
I will uphold you with my righteous right hand."
Have faith that the Lord your God is always near, for
even through the trials and tribulations of life, you
never walk alone. Isaiah 41

Lessons for The Soul

A Collection of Heartfelt

Devotionals with Journal

*But if from there you seek the
Lord your God, you will find
him if you seek him with all
your heart and with all your
soul. Gracious words are a
honeycomb, sweet to the soul
and healing to the bones.*

*Deuteronomy 4:29
Proverbs 16:24*

Single and Saved

A fter my divorce, I met the real me and embraced singleness. I have gained a lot in being single again, such as spending more time with God and praying more because this journey becomes challenging. Where God is taking us, we must have a consistent prayer walk and a multitude of faith to know that He will sustain. We must learn to endure despite the hardships. The enemy knows when you are stuck in your old life and your ancient form. If there are areas in your life that you have not healed in, it gives way for the enemy to infiltrate through the tiny holes.

God needs you to know that this is a special time when you are single, and a new season is calling you. God desires you to see what He sees in you, which is a perfect reflection of him. The Lord knows you will make mistakes, but He also uses your mistakes for your ministry.

Someone has gone through the same thing you have gone through and has not been able to make it. Tragic events will have you depressed, but you must pick yourself up. The enemy will tell you that you cannot be happy without him, and yet God will show you the splendidness of His wonders in your life.

Broken relationships

When, your children, ask you, "Momma, why did you stay?" With tears in your eyes, you must self-reflect and ask yourself that same question as to why you stayed so long. I had good and bad days within my marriage, but it is never a good idea to make excuses for why we remain in dysfunctional relationships. We always say it is for the children, but we think that we can't make it on our own. We also think that no man/woman will want to take care of you and your minor children. How can I make it financially with small children and be able to clothe, feed, and bathe them, while still taking care of the other necessities that come along with children?

If we think back over our life, we will see that we were doing everything and had everything we needed to survive while being financially and emotionally stable.

We must be empowered and know that God has us in every situation of our lives. We emotionally destroy loved ones when we think we are sheltering them from the pain when we are causing the pain.

Just like Frederick Douglas said, it is
easier to build strong children than to
repair broken men.

Let your children know you love them and that you can co-parent despite the differences you have and always put the children's needs first when it comes to a breakup. Do not turn the children against the other parent or talk down on the other parent in front of them. Children love both of their parents, and they should not have to feel as though they must choose one over the other one or made to feel shame for loving both of you. Do not ever tarnish the love they have for you in any way by harboring up bitter feelings for either parent. Keep the animosity down and try to have a civil relationship because it is better to walk in peace. Some will tell you that the older the children are, the easier it is for them to cope with heartache, but I know different. The older children see all the chaos in your relationship and are more observant than you realize.

Pray and hope that your children find mates that are the opposite of what they have witnessed. Find mates that will love them unconditionally by verbally expressing it and, most importantly, by showing it with actions.

Praise Out of Bondage

I was lying down in the bed, and I felt pinned down. I was immobilized, and I tried to open my mouth, and I could not even muster up a sound. I tried to call out to the Lord, and as soon as I said, "Lord Help," my voice became faint and then nothing.

I heard a voice saying sing, so I tried to sing "Glory, Glory, Hallelujah," my mouth was moving, but nothing was coming out. The voice came again and said sing, so I tried one more time and still no sound, no murmur, not nothing. The voice said, "Sing louder with more force." and when I did, all I could hear was a muffled sound. The voice spoke once more, saying, "Keep singing and do not stop." Suddenly, I was singing and could hear myself noticeably clear; I was literally yelling the words to the song, "I feel better, so much better since I laid my burdens down."

God will Carry you in a storm

I was in a car with another female who, at this time, I don't remember if it was someone I knew or not, there was a car full of children. Unsure on where we were, I just knew I was driving us back home to Arkansas. We were traveling a familiar way, and the road was underwater. We could not turn around because there were cars behind us. The children asked if we were going through the water, and I told them we did not have any other choice. I told everyone to brace themselves, and we started to pray and prayed continuously, and we went into the water then came out on the other side. God was with us in these instances because our car could have stalled while underwater. God was revealing himself to us that no matter the circumstances that he will be with us to protect us. In times of danger, call upon the Lord, and he will wrap his arms around you to comfort you and most definitely save you.

Hearing God's Voice

I remember that when I first heard the Lord speak to me, I thought I was going crazy. I listened to the most precise, distinctive voice ever. You must have an intimate relationship with God to know when he is talking with you. He gives clear and accurate instructions for us to do, but do we yield to them? We think that because we cannot see God that he does not know what we are doing, saying, or thinking, but that can't be further than the truth. We must get to a place where we are more worried about what God thinks of us than man.

God loves us, and he wants us to love one another also. I wake up with a positive attitude and a song in my heart every day. I love to sing because it is a way for me to release some afflictions that have me bound. You have to call out his name. JESUS… Like this song says, "There is no sweeter name, I know."

I have this saying, "Let your light shine, continually shine," and that is how we should be, so our lives will reflect the goodness of God. Let our light shine to bring some joy onto others. *Matthew 5: 5-14 NIV says: You are the light of the world. A town built on a hill cannot be hidden. Neither do people light a lamp and put it under a bowl. Instead, they put it on its stand, and it gives light to everyone in the house. In the same way, let your light shine before others, that they may see your good deeds and glorify your Father in heaven.*

When you have been under the anointing of God, it is the most fantastic thing you could ever experience. When we are in sin, it takes us from under our Fathers covering, and you will surely know it. It is similar to how a fish acts when they are no longer in the water. The fish flops around on the bank and gasps for air. I do not know how you act, but this is how I truly feel. Suffocating and gasping for air because my father is not answering me when I need him. In every aspect of our lives, God is right there with us, and he sees every smile and feels every turmoil. He will give us the solution to the problem if we only trust him through the process.

Coping with Death

A very dear friend of mine named Big-Will, whom I consider family, just happened to call me one day because he had lost one of his cousins. He asked me some startling questions which was, "Why God allowed him to still be living and breathing after making some terrible choices along the way, and other people he knew had not even gotten a ticket yet died?"

He wanted to know, "Why is it the people in his life who "Always" try to do the right thing suffer the most?" My friend wanted an explanation, and he went on to say that he buried so many people this year, Good people... yet they died. Death is inevitable, and it is time for families to come together, put aside or resolve differences, and show more love and compassion. *Like Ecclesiastes 3: 1-8 (NIV)says: There is a time for everything, and a season for every activity under the heavens: a time to be born and a time to die, a time to plant and a time to uproot, a time to kill and a time to heal, a time to tear down and a time to build, a time to weep and a time to laugh, a time to mourn and a time to dance, a time to scatter stones and a time to gather them, a time to embrace and a time to refrain from embracing, a time to search and a time to give up, a time to keep and a time to throw away, a time to tear and a time to mend, a time to be silent and a time to speak, a time to love and a time to hate, a time for war and a time for peace.*

My response: There is no explanation as to why life is unfair, but we as believers must know that God is in control, and there is a purpose in it all.

This conversation was so disheartening to me because when you know how good God is and not to understand why God lets us live and allow us to wake up every day was hard for me. I had to respond accordingly: We must tell the goodness of how God has been. Nobody wants to die or lose loved ones because we lose a piece of ourselves when this happens. *We just have to make sure we are loving everyone and performing God's law for us. John 14:15(NIV)*

Marital Advice

Take your spouse's feelings into consideration and alleviate the pain, especially if you are causing it. *If a problem arises yet, you do not address it and continue to let the hurt go on, then what does that say about your character?* That is not love nor respect, because a union of love that God has ordained for you is conscious of one's feelings and do everything; they can honor you.

The man who is the head of his family honors and cherishes his wife and does everything he possibly can to ensure that his wife is safe, loved, protected, and, most importantly, a priority. His actions showed he was no longer available mentally. It was not until my divorce that I understood what God meant when he said in *2 Corinthians 6:14: Do not be yoked together with unbelievers (NIV).* Even yoked individuals will have some discord at times but knowing that God is the head of your life and the head (Man) is responsible for the well-being of the family indeed sheds some light on things for me. Being married is more than two people saying they love one another or signing a marriage license. Love is also an action word. If you genuinely love the Lord, then you know that God requires you to have an Agape love. This is a selfless and unconditional love, which can weather through all kinds of seasons. Marriage will have its ups and downs, but most importantly, you will need to be able to forgive one another, respect one another, and serve one another and love one another.

When an individual's heart hardens, and they are no longer emotionally there, then the only thing that can even get you back on track is prayer.

Always Seek Wise Counsel

T he road was hard for my daughter, Larae, and I, but we were able to restore our relationship by attending and interacting in counseling. Prayer, in addition to counseling, helped a great deal. We are both wiser and healthier because of it. Mental issues are serious, and at times we don't want to deal with our problems because we think counseling isn't necessary. We would rather bury them and stay in denial than getting the urgent help that is needed.

I genuinely believe that if my daughter and I had not gone, then we may not have the fantastic relationship that we have now. With the help of a therapist and me continually praying to my father above for deliverance and healing, I know I would not have made it. God has blessed me with three girls, and I have had my share of heartaches with each of them.

I think God gives you children so you may understand what the actual concept of unconditional love is. Your children will have you crying because you don't want to see them hurt and go through many hardships, and then you cry because they have hurt you. This is all part of being a parent and loving them no matter what. Now I am sure that children have their way of thinking when it comes to us as parents and ensuring that communication plays a crucial component in fixing problems. Talk with each other when issues arise to keep the bitterness from festering, and if that does not work, then seek a professional mediator to help with the problems. Conflicts can be resolved, and healing takes place if you are willing to put in the work. I pray for all my children daily, even if they do not pray for themselves, to ensure that they are covered and protected.

About the Author

Paula Kendrick is a strong woman with fierce determination and perseverance. She has many roles, mother, sister, aunt, and grandmother, to name a few. Kendrick has been encouraging and offering words of inspiration along with much laughter to bless others by saying, "Continually Let Your Light Shine" and "Be Blessed and Be a Blessing." She has a heart as big as the Grand Canyon and will help anyone in need. She is a faithful servant at heart.

Living Water Books
Missions Statement

You trust your God-given vision in our hands, and it is our mission to connect, embrace, build, and breathe life into the writings that record all that God has allowed, inspired, and led you through. Your life is a story to be shared.

We spread the word of God from his heart through your hands and out into the world. God's living waters flowing through writings will cause lives to flourish and transform hearts with truth.

About the Publisher

Living Water Books is
A Christian Imprint of
Butterfly Typeface Publishing

*He who believes in me from his
Innermost being will flow continuously,
Rivers of Living Water. (John 7:38)*

https://livingwaterbooks.org/

Contact Us for All Your Publishing Needs

470-344-3891

www.ingramcontent.com/pod-product-compliance
Lightning Source LLC
Chambersburg PA
CBHW071836090426
42737CB00012B/2256